# Blest Are We
## Faith in Action

Thus faith comes from what is heard,
and what is heard comes through the word of Christ.

Romans 10:17

**Charley Cook**
Corporate Vice President
Kendall Hunt Publishing

**Anne P. Battes**
Publisher

**Mary Wessel**
Graphic Designer and Art Direction

## KINDERGARTEN
### STUDENT EDITION

RCL
Benziger

a Kendall Hunt Company
Cincinnati, Ohio

"The Subcommittee on the Catechism, United States Conference of
Catholic Bishops, has found this text, copyright 2019,
to be in conformity with the *Catechism of the Catholic Church*."

## Nihil Obstat Imprimatur

✝ Most Reverend Joseph R. Binzer
Auxiliary Bishop
Vicar General
Archdiocese of Cincinnati
March 26, 2018

The *nihil obstat and imprimatur* are official declarations that a book or pamphlet is free of doctrinal and moral error. No implication is contained therein that those who have granted the *nihil obstat* and *imprimatur* agree with the contents, opinion, or statements expressed.

## *Blest Are We* Faith in Action Team

**Contributing Writer**
Susan Traeger Gleason

**Theological Consultant**
Rev. Robert J. Hater, PhD

**Editorial Staff**
Mary Sellars Malloy, Project Manager
Karen Cain, Project Editor
Elizabeth Shepard, Project Editor

**Production Staff**
Bob Ishee, Production Manager

## *Blest Are We* Team

**Consultants**
Marlene McCabe, Cindy McNeil,
Madeline Sarli, S.S.J.

**Early Childhood Advisory Board**
Rev. Louis J. Cameli, S.T.D.,
Philip A. Cunningham,
Sister Clare Fitzgerald, S.S.N.D.,
William J. Freburger,
Greer G. Gordon,
Rev. Frank J. McNulty,
Janaan Manternach,
Carl J. Pfeifer

**National Catechetical Advisor**
Kathleen Hendricks

## Acknowledgments

All adaptations of Scripture are based on the *The New American Bible, Revised Edition* © 2010, 1991, 1970 Confraternity of Christian Doctrine, Inc., Washington, D.C.

Excerpts from the *Lectionary for Masses with Children*, copyright © 1993, United States Catholic Conference, Washington, D.C. Used with permission.

Excerpts from *Catholic Household Blessings and Prayers* (revised edition) © 2007, United States Conference of Catholic Bishops, Washington, D.C.

This work is protected by United States copyright laws and is provided solely for the use of teachers, catechists, and administrators in teaching and assessing student learning in their classes. Dissemination or sale of any part of this work (including the World Wide Web) will destroy the integrity of the work and is not permitted.

All content in this publication is protected by copyright. Permission should be obtained from the publisher prior to transmission in any form by any means, electronic, mechanical, photocopying, recording, or otherwise. For information regarding permission(s), write to: Permissions Department, RCL Benziger 8805 Governor's Hill Drive, Suite 220, Cincinnati, Ohio 45249. Blest Are We® is a trademark of RCL Benziger, a Kendall Hunt Company, or its affiliates.

Copyright © 2019 RCL Benziger, a Kendall Hunt Company. All Rights Reserved. Printed in the United States of America.

RCL Benziger
8805 Governor's Hill Drive • Suite 220
Cincinnati, OH 45249
Toll Free: 877-275-4725
Fax:        800-688-8356
Visit us at RCLBenziger.com

| | | |
|---|---|---|
| Textbook only: | 444830 | ISBN: 978-1-5249-4830-6 |
| Textbook with eBook: | 444828 | ISBN: 978-1-5249-4828-3 |

# Contents

# Welcome

# My Favorite Bible Story

Bible

This Bible belongs to

_____

- - - - - - - - - - - - - - - - - - - -

_____

# God Creates the Earth and Skies

# God's Gifts of Day and Night

God made the earth.

God gives me daytime and nighttime.

**Activity** Draw a ☀ or a ☽ in each box.

# Praise God for Earth and Sky

The Bible gives praise to God.
You can praise God, too!

6 Praise you, God,
for the stars at night.

Praise you, God,
for the sun. 3

Praise you, God, for . . .

My
Book of
Praise

8 Draw a picture here.

1

# Praise God

Psalm 136 praises God.

Praise you, God,
for the moon.

4

Praise you, God,
for the day.

5

Praise you, God,
for water.

2

Praise you, God,
for the earth.

7

FOLD ▶

# 🪔 God's Wonderful Creation

Pray this prayer.
It is from the Bible.

God created the wonderful  .

Thank you, God, for the .

God created the wonderful .

Thank you, God, for the .

God created the wonderful .

Thank you, God, for the .

God created the wonderful .

Thank you, God, for the .

God created the wonderful _____ .

Thank you, God, for the _____ .

God created the wonderful _____ .

Thank you, God for the _____ .

Thank you, God! Alleluia!

*Based on* Psalm 148:7-10, 14

## Dear Family,

Children are natural wonderers. Their enthusiasm helps you see God's world anew. As one young parent says, "I never want Amy to lose her ability to relax and enjoy things, so we go on 'being walks.' I follow Amy's lead, and we stop to pick up leaves, look at bugs, and trudge through fields. Together we celebrate the wonders of God's world." Share your love of God's creation with your child.

RCLBenziger.com

# God Creates the Animals

## Chapter 2

Circle the animal picture you like best.

# God Loves All the Animals

**Activity** Use the  to draw animals you like.

9

# God Gives Us Pets

We like to play with our pets.

How do you love and care for a pet?

**Activity** Draw a picture to show how.

## Thank God for Our Pets

Color God's name. Pray this prayer.

Thank you, God, for our wonderful pets.

# God Gives Us Animals to Love

**Activity** Draw one way you can care for each pet.

# God Made Animals

**Activity** Color the animals.

God made the animals that we see.

He made them for you and for me.

We thank God for our pets each day.

We care for and love them in every way.

We have fun when we play.

Hooray for God!

## Dear Family,

The children have been learning about God's wonderful gift of animals. They have learned that God gave us animals, and all gifts of creation, to care for and respect. If you have a family pet, welcome your child's efforts to help care for and feed your pet. Say a prayer with your child thanking God for all the animals. Ask God to help us take care of the animals and all of creation.

RCLBenziger.com

13

# God Creates People

## Chapter 3

Draw someone
God made and loves.

# God Loves Us

God

made

us.

God

loves

us.

15

# God Creates People Who Love Me

Sing this song to "Frère Jacques."

> Mommy, Daddy,
> baby Billy,
> they love me,
> they love me.
>
> Sister, friends, and Grandma,
> brother, aunt, and Grandpa,
> they love me,
> they love me.

**Activity** Look at the pictures. Circle one of them. Sing about it by adding a verse to the song.

# People Show Love

People are nice to us.

**Activity** Color the heart by your favorite picture.
Tell a story about the people in the picture.

# God Wants Us to Love Others

**Activity** Draw a ♡ by the ways you can love people.

# God's Love Creates a Wonderful World

**Activity** Draw some of God's gifts around your house.

## Dear Family,

Your child has completed Unit 1, which highlights the Scripture account of creation (see Genesis 1). You may want to read this story of creation to your child from a children's Bible. Then look at page 15 and trace the letters, "God made us. God loves us."

## 8

## Dear Family,

This storybook is based on Saint Francis of Assisi's stunning "Canticle of the Sun." It is the first take home storybook you will receive as part of the *Blest Are We Faith in Action* religion program.

While the ideas of "Canticle of the Sun" summarize the unit on creation, the book is meant to be a storybook. It is meant to be an enjoyable piece of literature.

It is also a prayer book. Notice that American Sign Language for the phrase "Praise God" is part of the prayer. Signing with your child whenever "Praise God" appears in the text will make the reading more prayerful.

You might want to teach your child an additional canticle verse, such as: *For all creation I make this prayer and promise for the earth to care.*

Name _____

My Take-Home Storybook

canticle of the SUN

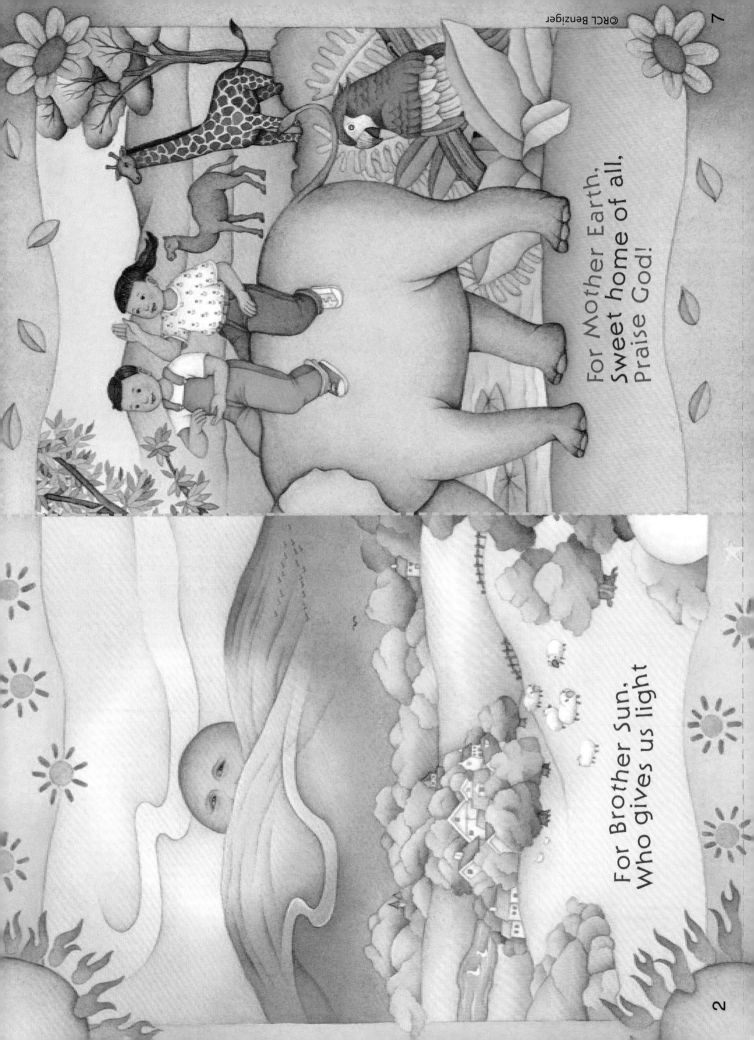

For Mother Earth,
sweet home of all.
Praise God!

For Brother Sun,
Who gives us light

For every creature,
Great and small

For Sister Moon,
And the stars of night,
Praise God!

Praise

God

6

3

For Sister Water,
Who fills the seas.
Praise God!

For Brother Wind,
Who gives us breeze

5

4

# God Creates Me

## Chapter 4

I am special

You are a gift from God.
Draw your picture here.

# God Creates Me Special

Show what is special about you.

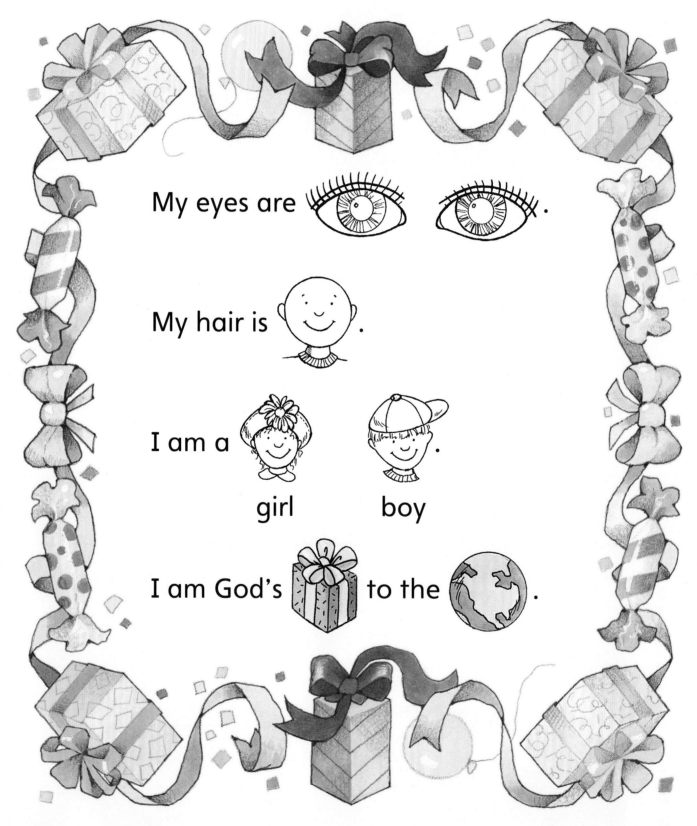

My eyes are    .

My hair is    .

I am a    .

girl     boy

I am God's   to the   .

# God Gives Me Many Talents

**Activity** Circle what you can do.

# God Helps Me Learn New Things

**Activity** Put the pictures in 1, 2, 3 order.

I can watch people to learn how to do things.

I can do things over and over to learn.

27

# 🪔 I Can Praise the Lord with My Talents

Color the name of the Lord.

Then pray this prayer with your class.
The response is from Psalm 146 in the Bible.

Praise the 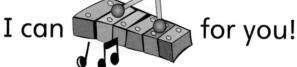 LORD, my soul; . . .

I can  for you!

When the ☀️ comes up,

You 🖤 me.

I am glad I am your child.

Praise the  LORD, my soul; . . .

I can praise you with music!

Praise the LORD, my soul; . . .

When the  comes up,

God's ♥ will be with me.

You make me happy, God!

Praise the LORD,

my soul; . . .

*Response:* Psalm 146:2

## Dear Family,

Every child is gifted. Some children draw especially well; others tell good stories. Some display agility and good coordination; others can take things apart and put them back together with ease. No matter what your child can do or cannot do, he or she is a gift from God. Take time to recognize and to show appreciation for your child's gifts, and help him or her build upon them. Discuss with your child two gifts that he or she possesses. Then watch when that gift is shared this week and recognize your child in a special way.

RCLBenziger.com ✝

# God Gives Me Feelings

# Happy

God wants us to be happy.

Color the word "Happy."

# God Knows When We Are Sad

**Activity** Color the word "Sad."

Draw yourself helping someone who is sad.

# God Knows How We Feel

Tell how the children feel.

**Activity** Draw the way you might feel next to each picture.

# We Can Share Our Feelings

Do you ever feel like these children?

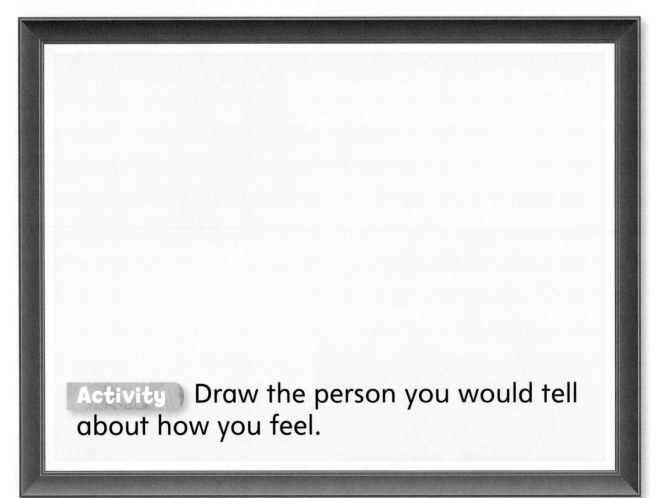

**Activity** Draw the person you would tell about how you feel.

# Mary Was Happy When Jesus Was Found

Listen to the Bible story. It is The Finding of Jesus in the Temple from Luke 2:41-52.

Then color the picture of Jesus and his parents by the Temple.

## Mary's Prayer

My  praises God.

I am 🙂 .

My son 👦 was lost.

But 🧔 and I found 👦 safe.

👦 was talking to the teachers and 🙏 .

Now 👦 is home and we are a family.

I will remember all that 👦 does in my 💜 .

God has blessed me and I am 🙂 .

## Dear Family,

Jesus' parents worried about him when he was lost in the Temple. When they found him, they were filled with joy. Your child wants to share his or her happy feelings as well as his or her worries with you. Help your child know that he or she is a source of happiness to you, and that you will share in his or her feelings. Add to your child's feelings of self-worth by being a good listener.

RCLBenziger.com ✝

# God Gives Us Senses

## Chapter 6

We use our senses every day.

How do our senses help us?

# My Senses Help Me Enjoy God's World

My senses are gifts from God.

**Activity** Cut out the pieces. Enjoy the puzzle.

# God Wants Us to Use Our Senses

My senses help me learn about God's world.

**Activity** Make the storybook about senses.

He felt the fleece of a tiny lamb.
He got all wet when the
dolphin swam!

6

He heard a tiger roar real loud.
He heard the laughter of the crowd.

3

**Dear Family,** Your child is learning about God's gift of the senses. At home, you and your family can play games using the senses. For example, to play a hearing game, hide objects that make sounds (a bell, whistle, timer, or drum). Whoever finds one can sound it. For the smelling game, put spices such as pepper, cinnamon, or oregano into bags and let your family identify the spices by smelling them. Play a sight-touch game in one room of the house. Whoever is "it" gives clues describing the object. The winner touches the object to identify it. At the end of each game say, "Thank you, God."

8 *RCLBenziger.com*

Tyler and His Senses

1

# My Storybook About Senses

He smelled the food the monkeys ate.

They never even used a plate!

4

He stopped to eat a tasty snack, Some yummy peanuts in a sack.

5

Tyler went to the zoo today.

He saw a snake whose name was Mae.

2

Tyler could see and hear and play.

Make a drawing of his fine zoo day!

Thank you, God for today!          7

# Thank God for My Senses

Activity Draw a line to finish the sentence.

I can feel a      !
Thank you, God, for my •

I can see the     !
Thank you, God, for my •

I can hear the     !
Thank you, God, for my •

I can taste the     !
Thank you, God, for my •

I can smell the     !
Thank you, God, for my •

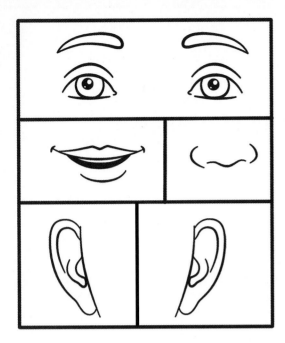

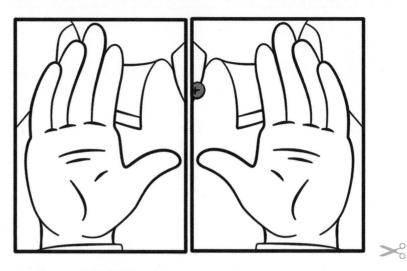

**Activity** Cut out the parts.
Glue them in their places.
Add hair and color.

You made me
wonderful!
Thank you, God!

41

# Dear Family,

The booklet *Just Like Me* features the exuberant five-year-old Jason Patrick Rochester Dundee. He expresses his own specialness. And he is proud of his accomplishments, as kindergartners usually are.

As you enjoy this book with your child, point out his or her abilities to name and share feelings and to recognize and develop talents. Remember: Absolutely no one is exactly like your child! God made your child unique.

When your child brings home this storybook, read it together several times. Afterwards, you might show your child how to cut along the blue lines found in the middle of pages 3–6.

Demonstrate how to flip the pages back and forth to enjoy the many faces that belong to Jason Patrick Rochester Dundee. Then ask your child to share his or her many faces!

Name _____

©RCL Benziger

## My Take-Home Storybook

Your feelings, gifts, and senses
Give you the chance to be
The special you that's only you —

Just like Me!

---

My name is Jason Patrick
Rochester Dundee.
No one that you've ever met is

Just like Me!

**6**

I have the sense to listen,
To taste, touch, smell, and see.
All my senses help to keep me

# Just Like Me!

# Just Like Me!

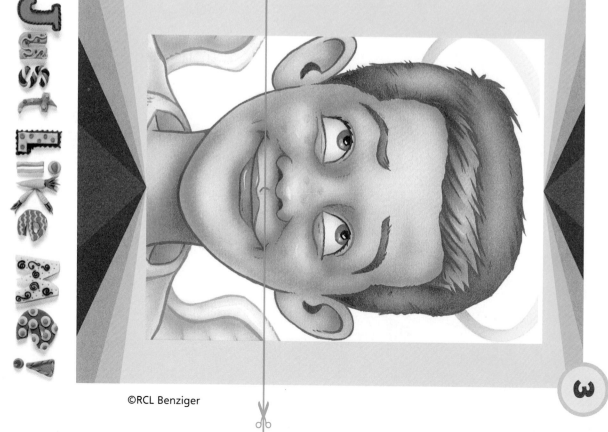

Yup, I am very special,
As you can plainly see.
No one in the whole wide world looks

**3**

©RCL Benziger

I have my own true feelings,
Like joy, surprise, and glee.
No one who has ever felt feels

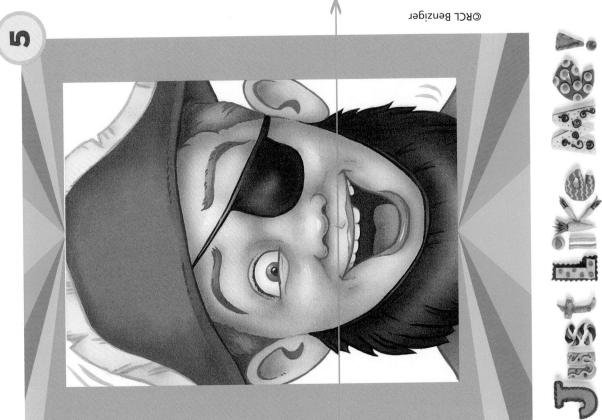

Just like Me!

I can do all sorts of things!
And this I'll guarantee,
No one else will ever do them

Just like Me!

# God Gives Us Families

## Chapter 7

Circle the picture that looks most like your family.

# God Makes My Family Special

A family is a sign of God's love.
My family is God's gift to me!

Draw your family here.

## Dear Family,

Your patient love helps your child develop his or her personality. By asking about your child's thoughts, feelings, and experiences, and by respecting his or her emerging opinions, you show that your child is important to you. To help your child share with you, sit together and tell funny stories about your own childhood and family. Talk about the ways your family cares for one another. Invite your child to take pictures of your family. Together, with your child, post them or text to family members.

RCLBenziger.com ✝

# The Loving Father

God is like a loving father. Jesus told this story about a loving father. Listen carefully.

Put the pictures in 1, 2, 3, 4 order.

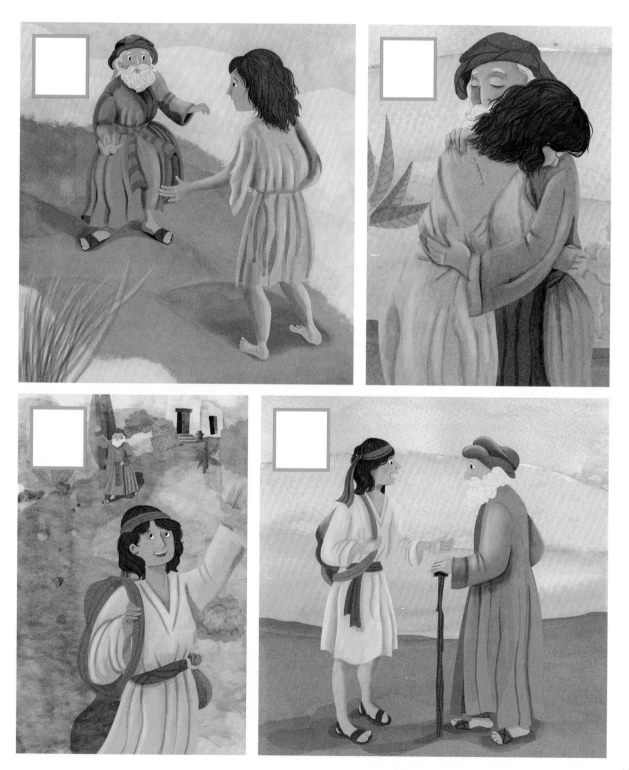

# Loving My Family

My **Family** loves me.

My **Family** cares for me.

I love my **Family** .

I care for my **Family** .

# God Gives Us Friends

## Chapter 8

Draw a picture
of a friend.

# A Thank You Prayer for Friends

Color the letters.

Now pray for your friends.

My play friends love me. Thank you, God!

My small friends love me. Thank you, God!

My friends love me. Thank you, God!

# God Likes Us to be Good Friends

**Activity** Play the game Be A Good Friend.

Flip a penny.
Heads = Move 1 time.
Tails = Move 2 times.

Start

Invite a friend. 1

Share fun. 2

Go back one. 3

Care. 4

Help.

5

Share toys. 6

We are friends. 7

54

# Our Wonderful Friends

God's love cares for us.

God's love cares for our friends.

God asks us to love our friends.

How can you tell these children are friends?

## Dear Family,

Friends help your child know and accept that he or she is lovable and likeable. It is helpful if you can provide opportunities for your child to meet a range of friends: some older, some the same age, and people of all cultures and nationalities. Each can enrich your child's life, and in this way you can help your child appreciate the diverse gifts of God's love. Say a prayer to thank God for friends.

RCLBenziger.com ✝

# God Gives Us Teachers

Teachers help us learn. They help us learn about God. Teachers are like friends, too.

Jesus

6

Coach

3

Helping your child understand that teachers and catechists have an important role in your family is critical. Since you are the primary teacher of your child, teachers and catechists help you by sharing the knowledge of the faith and being witnesses as disciples of Jesus Christ. They are friends of Jesus, your family, and your child. With your child, think of ways that you can show appreciation of your child's teacher or catechist. Then decide on one way and share that appreciation with your child's teacher or catechist to celebrate his or her commitment to you, your family, and especially to your child.

**Dear Family,**

8  RCLBenziger.com ✝

Thank You, God, for Teachers.

1

# My Teacher Book

We thank God for our teachers.

**Activity** Make the book about teachers.

My Kindergarten Teacher

4 Draw your teacher here.

World Language Teacher

5

peace
paz
paix
nabadda

Dance Teacher

Religion Teacher

2

7

# God Gives Us Neighbors

## Chapter 9

God gives us helpers to care for us.

Draw yourself listening to the firefighters.

# Neighbors Help Us

God wants us to help others.
Color the helpers you see.

HOLY NAME SCHOOL

MAIN ST.

**Activity** Draw yourself helping others.

# We Can Visit Neighbors

**Activity**   Start at the school.
Use your finger to go places.

# My Prayer for Neighbors

Thank you, God, for
Please care for them.

Thank you, God, for
Please care for them.

Thank you, God, for
Please care for them.

Thank you, God, for
Please care for them.

Thank you, God, for _____ .

Amen.

## Dear Family,

After watching a neighbor weed her perennial garden, a child may strike up a conversation at dinner about how seeds grow into flowers. Such a neighbor has widened the child's horizon. Chat with your child to discover all the helpful people in his or her immediate world. Use the finger puppets on page 62 of your child's book and retell the story of the Good Samaritan from Luke 10:29-37. Discuss how neighbors can help each other in many different ways. Pray for your neighbors and ask God to bless them.

RCLBenziger.com ✝

# Neighbors Share God's Love

**Activity** Use finger puppets to tell the story of the Good Samaritan.

Make finger puppets of the people in the Bible story.

# The Story of the Good Samaritan

Cut out all the finger puppets.
Glue the tabs together to make
the finger puppets.

Name _____

## Dear Family,

This story can help your child better recognize that family, friends, teachers, neighbors, and others support him or her with their love. Your child can reach out to others with love, too.

This humorous story encourages your child to be aware of others outside the family who can help him or her. But it is to family, in particular, that your child looks most consistently for the supportive love that is so necessary for the growth and development. Nourished and sustained by your love, your child is enabled to appreciate that love and to reach out with love to others. In this way your child grows in his or her love for God and others.

©RCL Benziger

**My Take-Home Storybook**

# Wanda Wondered Why

"Wow!" said Wanda.
"That's just what I thought.
But I was just wondering."

Wanda wondered,
"Why did God give me a family?
My family is neat, but I wonder.
Why not grow up in a zoo or a jungle?
"Why?" wondered Wanda.

"Why, Wanda!" said Mom with wonder.
"You have family and friends.
You have neighbors and teachers.
God gave them to you to love you.
And God wants you to love them!"

©RCL Benziger

"Why did God give me teachers?
Why can't I learn things all by myself?"
Wanda wondered.

A
B
C
D

5

"Why did God give me friends and neighbors?
I know they can be helpful.
I know they can be fun, " said Wanda.
"But why can't I have fun all by myself?"

4

# Jesus Is Born

Signs remind us of special days.

Draw a sign
of your birthday.

# Signs of God's Love

**Activity** Circle the signs of God's love.

## Dear Family,

Christians believe that mystery and meaning abound in life. Thus, we employ symbols. As an example, you hug your child and mean, "I love you." You listen to your kindergartner's story and mean, "I am interested in you." This week your child learned that Jesus is God the Father's greatest gift of love. Like God the Father, give your child many signs of your love.

RCLBenziger.com

# God the Father Sends His Son

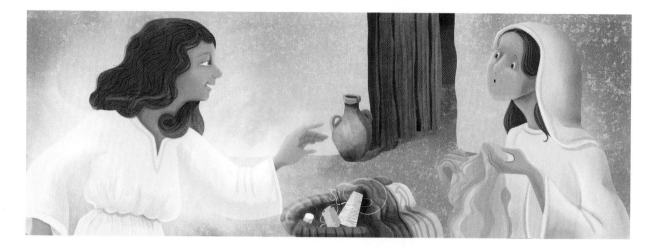

**Storyteller:** The angel Gabriel was sent from God
to a town in Galilee called Nazareth.
The angel was sent to share
God's message with Mary.

**Angel:** Hail, favored one!
The Lord is with you.

Do not be afraid, Mary.
You will bear a son,
and you shall name him Jesus.
He will be called holy, the Son of God.

**Mary:** I am the handmaid of the Lord.
May it be done to me
according to your word.

*Based on* Luke 1:26-28,30,35,38

# Jesus Is God's Son

Jesus is God's special sign of love.

**Activity** Color every shape that has an X in it.

# Jesus Shows Us God's Love

**Activity** Make a chain to celebrate Jesus' love.

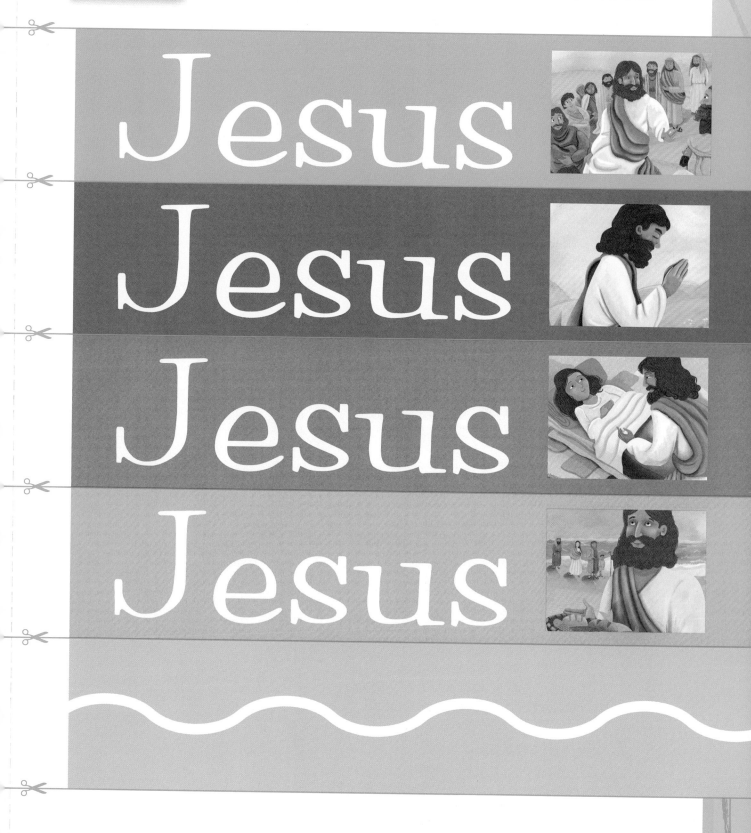

# We Can Show God's Love

We love God.

## Chapter 11

# Jesus Gathers Friends

Count the children who are acting like friends.

# Friends of Jesus Follow Him

Listen to a Bible story from the Gospel of Matthew.

Jesus walked by the Sea of Galilee.

He saw two brothers.

Their names were Peter and Andrew. They were fishermen.

Jesus said to them, "Come after me."

"I will make you fishers of men."

*Based on* Matthew 4:18-19

# Jesus Is Our Friend

Jesus' new friends went with him. They helped him gather friends.

**Activity**

Finish coloring the fish.

Jesus is a friend.

I am a friend of Jesus.

Jesus gathers friends.

**Activity** Cut out the fish. Make a mobile.

Jesus is a friend.

I am a friend of Jesus.

Jesus gathers friends.

# The Friends of Jesus Gather at Mass

The Catholic Church is the family of God.
The family of God gathers on Sunday.
We praise and thank God together.

**Activity** Draw you and your family coming to Mass.

# The Friends of Jesus Pray at Mass

**Activity** Color the crosses.

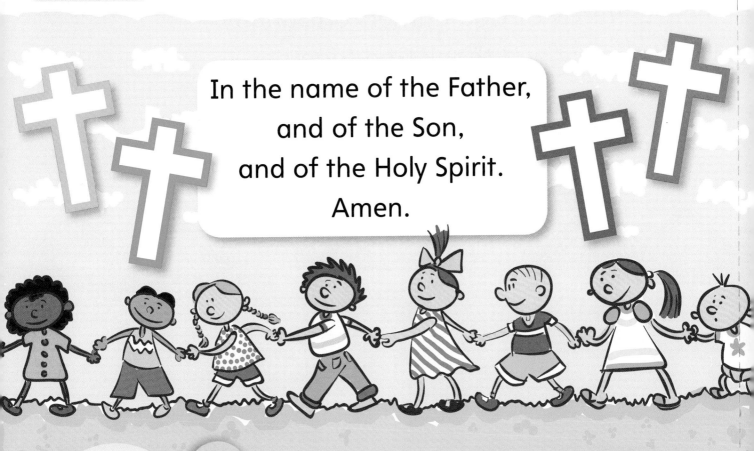

In the name of the Father,
and of the Son,
and of the Holy Spirit.
Amen.

## Dear Family,

Help your child discover that the friends of Jesus reach out to others. Choose an evening to listen to your child tell stories about Jesus, then share a story that you remember about Jesus. Together you can discover how Jesus knew more about friendship and love than anyone who ever walked on the earth. Explain to your child that we continue to learn about Jesus at Mass. The next Sunday your family attends Mass, listen for the stories about Jesus. Talk about those stories as a family.

RCLBenziger.com ✝

# Jesus Tells Stories

## Chapter 12

## An Add-On Story

**Al Gator** was very friendly.

He took his friends for rides.

They sat on his big strong back.

Down the river they glided.

**Lady Bug** was one of Al's friends.

She offered to fly off to get lunch.

She came back with berries and nuts.

The riders all enjoyed a picnic.

**Tammy Turtle** came along, too.

"This is great!" she said.

"I think I'll hop off for a swim."

What do you think happened to Tammy?

Add the next exciting part to the story.

# The Bible Is God's Holy Book

God gave us the Bible. We read about God and creation in the Bible. We read about Jesus in the Bible.

**Activity**

Trace the name of God's book and decorate it.

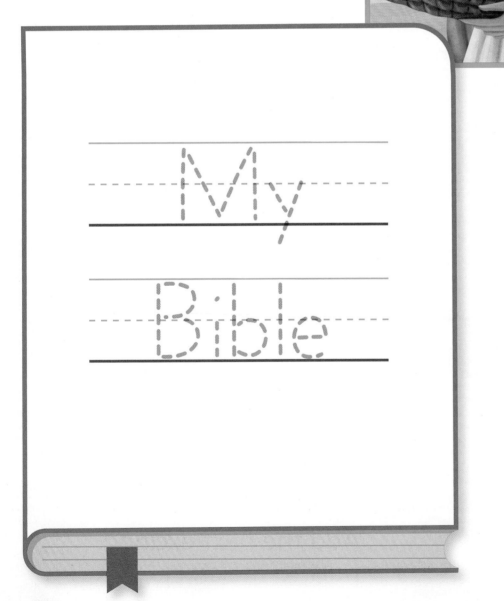

# Jesus Tells About a Lost Sheep

Help the shepherd find the lost sheep.

**Activity** Finish drawing the line to the lost sheep.

# A Story About Being Found

Connect the dots.
Color the word.

83

# We Sing Alleluia at Mass

**Activity** Add glitter to this happy word.

# Alleluia

# We Listen to Jesus' Stories at Mass

**Activity** Draw yourself listening to a story of God's love.

## Dear Family,

The story we share with our children is a love story. Like God, we love our children now and always. To show how much you have always loved your child, tell stories about when he or she was a toddler. What made you laugh? What made you fearful? What made you text a friend to say, "Do you know what my little one just did?" Now, share the stories of Jesus together!

RCLBenziger.com

# Jesus Gives Thanks

## Chapter 13

## 🪔 Healing the Blind Beggar

Listen to a Bible story from the Gospel of Luke.

**1** A blind man was sitting by the roadside begging.

The crowd told him, "Jesus of Nazareth is passing by."

**2** The blind man shouted, "Jesus, Son of David, have pity on me!"

**3** Jesus told him, "Have sight.

Your faith has saved you."

**4** The blind man received his sight and gave glory to God.

*Based on* Luke 18: 35, 37, 38, 42-43

**Activity** Finish coloring what the man said.

# Thank you, God!

**Dear Family,**

God calls us friends and fills our lives. An appropriate response is that of thanksgiving. Help your child discover ways to express thanksgiving. You might show him or her a memento given to you by a loved one and talk about why you are thankful for that memento. Share what it means to you. Invite your child to hold the memento and to ask questions. Then encourage your child to share something for which he or she is thankful, and to explain why.

RCLBenziger.com ✦

# Jesus Thanks God the Father

**Activity** Draw a line to what Jesus might have thanked God the Father for.

# We Can Thank God, Too

**Activity** Write a letter to God. Cut out what you are thankful for. Glue the pictures in the squares.

Dear God,

Thank you for

Thank you for

Thank you for

Love,

_____

Your Name

# Places We Can Thank God

**Activity** Put an **X** where you can thank God.

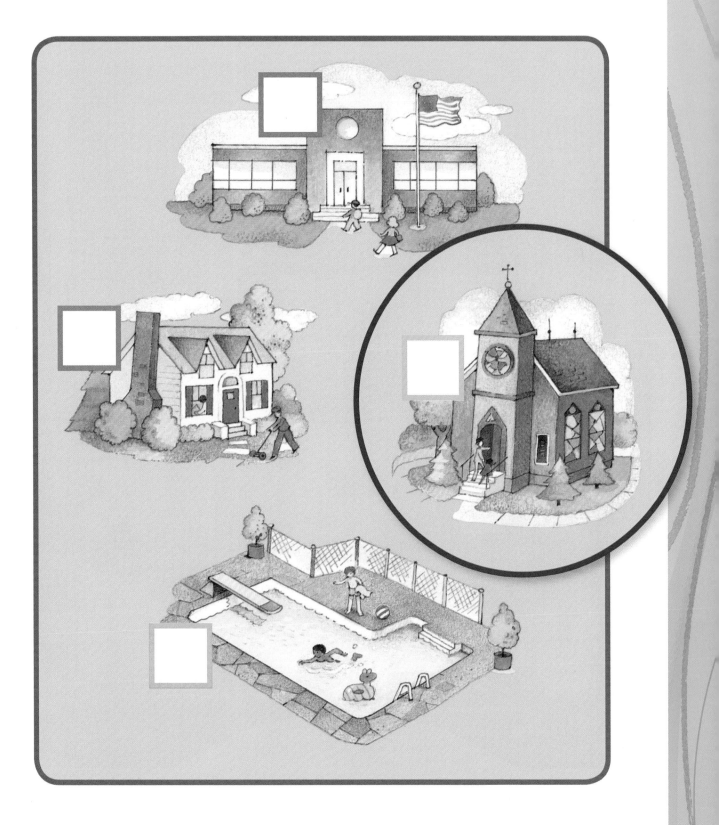

## We Can Thank God at Mass

Thank you, God, for all your love.

**Activity** Color the words.

# Jesus Celebrates

What's wrong with this birthday celebration?

# We Celebrate

Activity Match the food with the celebration.

# Jesus Celebrates with a New Friend

This play is based on a story from the Gospel of Matthew.

Storyteller   Jesus   Matthew   People

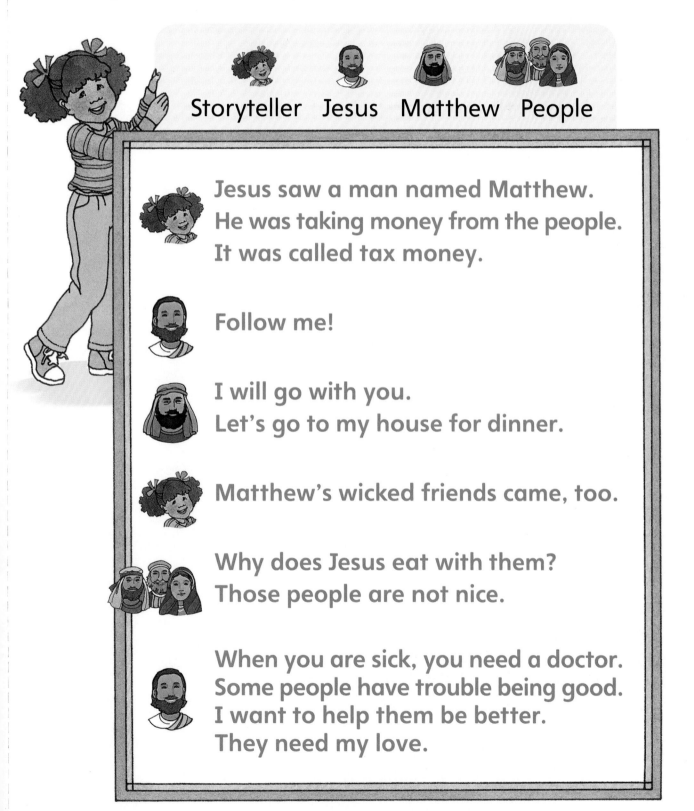

Jesus saw a man named Matthew.
He was taking money from the people.
It was called tax money.

Follow me!

I will go with you.
Let's go to my house for dinner.

Matthew's wicked friends came, too.

Why does Jesus eat with them?
Those people are not nice.

When you are sick, you need a doctor.
Some people have trouble being good.
I want to help them be better.
They need my love.

*Based on* Matthew 9:9-13

Learn these words that Jesus said.

. . . "Follow me."

Matthew 9:9

## Dear Family,

You can teach your child that there is much to celebrate in life. Jesus calls all of us to follow him and to come to know God's love. God has great love for us, and in the light of that love, you can celebrate. Laugh, sing, eat, and lift up your hearts! Take a walk with your child. (Or go sledding, skating, skiing, or swimming!) As you walk, experience God's wonders together. Go home and celebrate. Have a treat! Sing a song! Laugh! Trust God's love.

RCLBenziger.com

# Jesus Celebrates with All His Friends

**Activity** Color the picture of Jesus.

# We Can Celebrate with Jesus

The priest helps us pray at Mass.

**Activity** Finish coloring the priest's vestment red.

# Jesus Lives God's Love

## Chapter 15

See how Jesus loves others.

Some children are showing love, too.

Some are forgetting about others.

Put an X over the forgetful pictures.

# We Can Show Love

**Activity** Circle what you can use to show love.

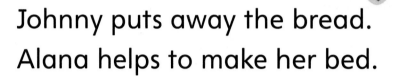

Johnny puts away the bread.
Alana helps to make her bed.

Colin sweeps the kitchen clean.
Sophie keeps the garden green.

Jack bakes a cake to eat.
Sarah keeps her crayons neat.

They all help and show they care.
Here and there and everywhere!

When we care we share God's love.
Live like Jesus, God's beloved.

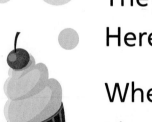

# Jesus Shares God the Father's Love

Follow the path to the pictures of Jesus.

**Activity** Tell stories about how Jesus is sharing his love with others.

# We Know How to Love

**Activity** Circle these words in the puzzle. Then read the message.

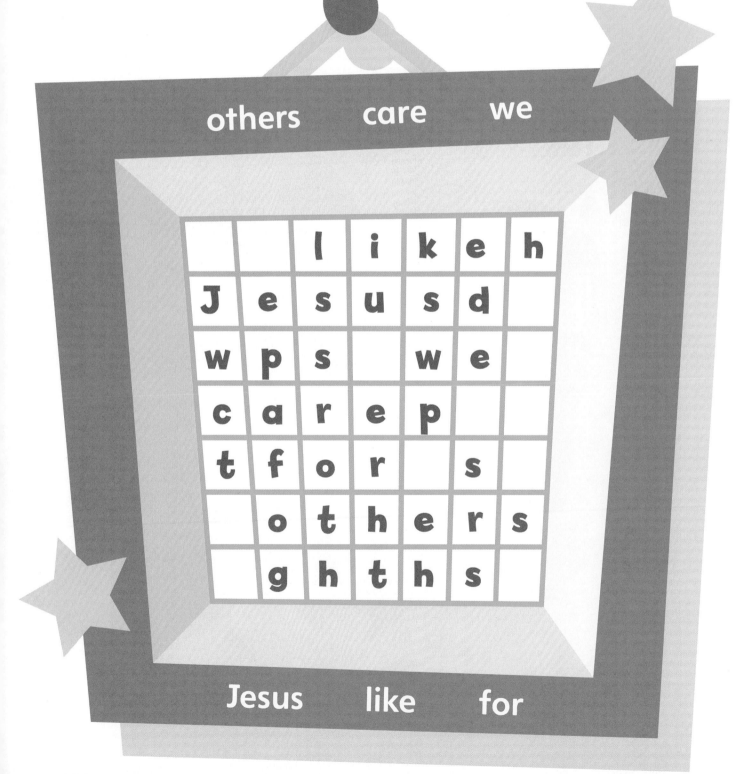

others    care    we

| | | l | i | k | e | h |
| J | e | s | u | s | d | |
| w | p | s | | w | e | |
| c | a | r | e | p | | |
| t | f | o | r | | s | |
| | o | t | h | e | r | s |
| | g | h | t | h | s | |

Jesus    like    for

101

# We Thank God at Mass

**Activity** Make the Mass booklet.

We pray the Lord's Prayer.
We share a sign of peace.

6

We stand and sing Alleluia.

3

**Dear Family,** Help your child understand that God's love comes to him or her through people: teachers, priests, the bus driver, the clerk at the grocery store, the friend next door, and, most importantly, parents and families. You are God's presence for your child. And remember God is present to you, too, in your child.

For these gifts and all of God's gifts to us, we celebrate and give thanks to God at Mass. Your child may use this booklet to help him or her participate in the Mass.

8

*RCLBenziger.com* ✝

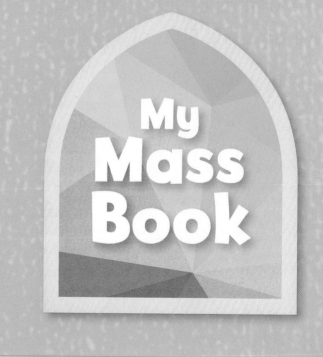

My Mass Book

# We Learn about God at Mass

We listen to the Gospel.
It tells the story of Jesus.

4

We give thanks in Jesus' name.

5

The friends of Jesus gather.
We pray the Sign of the Cross.

2

We receive Holy Communion.
We say, "Amen."

7

## Dear Family,

Children's great capacity for wonder serves them well during times of prayer. Ritual actions, symbols, and the beautiful language of Scripture and prayer help children absorb the awe it is meant to convey. Naturally, they do not understand every word individually, but they experience the sense of the holy.

This booklet attempts to create a sense of awe by using the language of the Bible to express the wonder of liturgical prayer celebrated with the People of God, the Church.

Impressive spaces also have a profound effect on children, and the church is no exception. Children realize it is the house of God. Young children love to explore, and one of the most interesting places to take them is to the church. With your child, walk around your parish church and examine some of the holy things in it.

Name _____

# I Go to the House of the Lord

My Take-Home Storybook

1

# In a Holy Place

**paschal candle**

2017 Ω

**ambo**

**stained-glass**

**statue of Mary**

How lovely is your dwelling. O Lord of hosts!

Psalm 84:2

Bless the LORD, my soul!

*Based on Psalm 103:1*

## Holy Things

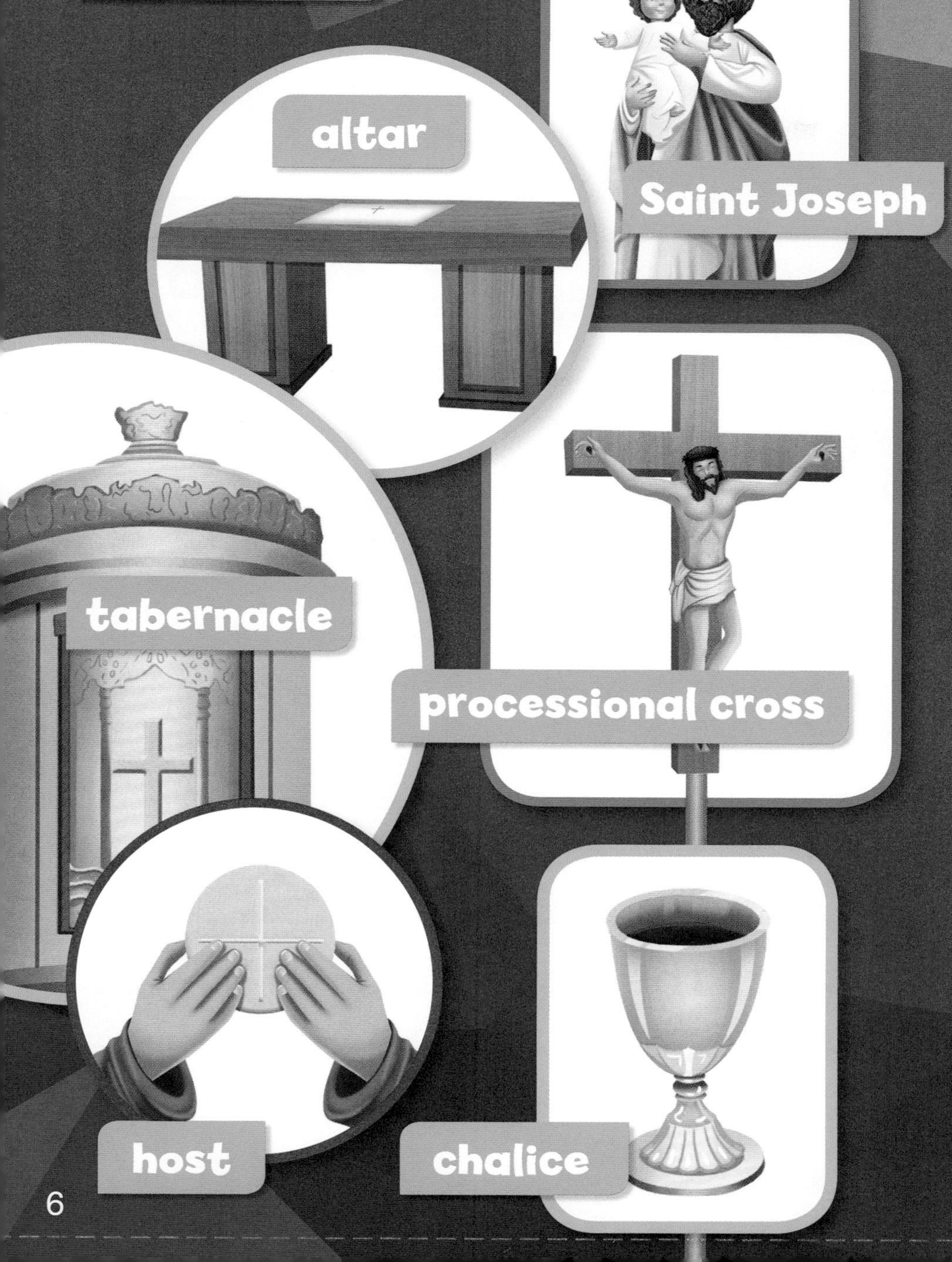

host

tabernacle

altar

chalice

processional cross

Saint Joseph

# Bless his holy name!

*Based on Psalm 103:1*

The Lord's mercy is from age to age.

*Based on Psalm 103:17*

Do not forget all his gifts.

*Based on Psalm 103:2*

# God Loves Us

## Chapter 16

## Water is Important

Connect the dots
to finish the pictures.

# Water Helps Us Care!

How have you used water to care?

**Activity** Mark an X by the pictures that show what you can do.

# We Celebrate Baptism

God calls us to be Jesus' friends forever.
We become friends of Jesus at Baptism.
We belong to the Catholic Church.

**Activity** Color the water blue.

# The Friends of Jesus Welcome Us

The friends of Jesus clap and clap.
Clap! Clap! Clap!
Welcome!

Clap for a new child of God.

## Dear Family,

Your child was introduced to the Sacrament of Baptism. This would be an appropriate time to show your child's baptismal pictures or video, and to display the white garment and the candle he or she received during the celebration of this Sacrament. Consider lighting the candle for supper and inviting your family to pray, "Thank you, God, for making us special friends of Jesus."

RCLBenziger.com

# We Are God's Children

## 🪔 God Loves All Children

Jesus had walked all day.
He was tired and sat on a rock.
He taught people about God.

People brought their children to Jesus.
They wanted Jesus to bless them.
The children wanted to be with Jesus.

Some grown-ups shouted.
They said, "Go away! Jesus is tired."

But Jesus did not shout.
He smiled at the children.
Jesus said, "Let them be!
Let the children come to me."
Jesus hugged the children.
Jesus blessed them.

*Based on* Matthew 19:13-15

**Activity** Draw yourself in the picture with Jesus.

# God Makes Us Alike But Different

**Activity** Follow the maze to school.
Stop at each place and look around.
What are the children doing?

Talk about some of the same things you do.

# Children Belong to God

**Activity** Color the picture of one of God's children.

# God's Children Can Have Fun

**Activity** What do you think is the most fun? Put a check ✓ in one of the balloons.

**Activity** Look at the pictures of God's children. Put an **X** in the hands to show what you want to learn.

## Dear Family,

God's love is freely given to us. There are no conditions. To imitate God's love, resist insisting that your child earn your love by doing prescribed actions. Offer love and support as your child attempts to learn new behavior. To talk about love to your child, retell the story of his or her birth and describe how you felt.

*RCLBenziger.com* ✝

# We Love Others

## Chapter 18

Write the first letters of your friends' names on the flowers.

God Loves Us

God Loves Others

# Jesus Tells Us About God

Jesus is God's Son.

Jesus told the people about God.

**Activity** Draw yourself listening to Jesus.

What do you think Jesus could be saying?

122

# We Love to Hear Stories About Jesus

**Activity** Cut out the story wheel.
Spin the wheel to pick a picture.
Then tell the story about Jesus.

## We Love Jesus' Goodness

Jesus, Mary, and his disciples were at a wedding.

The wedding was in Cana.

The host ran out of wine.

Mary said to Jesus, "They have no wine."

Jesus told the servants, "Fill the jars with water.

Draw out some water and take it to the headwaiter."

The servants did so.

**Activity** Tell what you think happened next.

The headwaiter tasted the water that had become wine.

He told the groom, "Everyone serves good wine first.

But you have kept the good wine until now." In doing this, Jesus showed his glory.

Jesus' disciples began to believe in him.

*Based on John 2:3, 7, 9, 10*

Did you guess right?

YES ☐    NO ☐

## Dear Family,

Your child's class is preparing a play about the wedding at Cana. You are invited to join us in the creative, imaginative, and fun-filled world of your child. Celebrate with him or her the Good News that God is love; celebrate the Gospel message that Jesus came to show us love. Come to the play prepared to watch your child enjoy the Good News!

RCLBenziger.com

## Dear Family,

This story is one of encouragement. It reminds your child that he or she can do many things and share many blessings. The story can also help your child share his or her talents and blessings with you and with others. During this year, your child has been growing in many ways and most especially growing in faith. His or her development has, in a way, been a gift to you. You treasure your child's small proclamations of faith and generous sharing of talents. Encourage him or her to continue to grow in faith and to share with others. These are two wonderful traits to pursue.

Name _____

©RCL Benziger

My Take-Home Storybook

# If Tammy Toucan Can, You Can

7

Tammy Toucan can celebrate.
And if Tammy Toucan can, you can.

This is Tammy Toucan.
She lives in a high, jungle tree.

2

6

Tammy can share with her family.
She can help her friends.

Tammy loves to share and care.
And if Tammy Toucan can, you can.

©RCL Benziger

3

5

She can screen herself from the sun
and take care of herself.
And if Tammy Toucan can, you can.

4  Tammy Toucan can eat healthy foods.
She can keep herself clean.

# Jesus Helps Us Say We Are Sorry

## Chapter 19

Color the faces.

# I Get Along With Others

Draw yourself playing with friends.

131

# I Am Sorry

We make choices.

Sometimes we make a wrong choice.

Jesus helps us to say we are sorry.

# We Forgive Others

**Activity** Draw one way you would show you are sorry.

## Dear Family,

You are your child's first and best example of God's never-ending love. You are also the model of forgiveness for your child. When your child does something wrong, remind him or her that even though you don't love the action, you will always love your child. Then show forgiveness by sharing quality time together: take a walk, read a book, or play a game. Remind your child that God will help us make good choices. We can live as children of God.

RCLBenziger.com

# Jesus Teaches Us About Love

Jesus taught us that God loves us.
We must love God, ourselves, and others.

## Love God and Others

Love God with your whole .
Love others as much as you love yourself.

**Activity** Color the word love.

135

# The Holy Spirit Helps Us

## Chapter 20

Draw one more thing the wind can do.

# The Holy Spirit

The Holy Spirit is like the wind.

**Activity** Color the words.

Holy Spirit

# Jesus Promises the Holy Spirit

It was time for Jesus to live with God the Father in Heaven.

Jesus promised to send the Holy Spirit.

The Holy Spirit would fill people with Good News.

# Come, Holy Spirit

Listen to this story.

**Activity**  Finish the story by coloring the pictures.

Jesus' friends were  .

The Holy Spirit came to them.

The Holy Spirit was like a strong  .

The Holy Spirit filled them with God's .

The Holy Spirit helped them. Jesus' friends told everyone the Good News about God!

# The Holy Spirit Helps Us

**Activity** Draw a picture of how the Holy Spirit helps you.

# Symbols of the Holy Spirit

**Activity** Connect the dots.

## Dear Family,

Your child is learning that God is always with each of us. God the Holy Spirit helps us to learn about Jesus and to pray. Share stories with your child of times when God has helped you. Pray together when there is a special need in your family. Read the Bible together and talk about your favorite Bible stories. Help your child understand that you are always trying to listen to God's word in your own life. Pray together, "Come, Holy Spirit, fill our hearts with love. Amen."

RCLBenziger.com ✝

# Jesus Taught Us to Pray

## Chapter 21

We talk
to our friends.

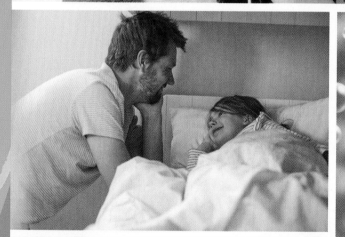

# We Pray to God

When we pray we are talking to God.

**Activity** Share how you pray to God.

# Our Father

We learn to pray the Our Father.

**Activity** Make your prayer book.

and lead us not into temptation,
but deliver us from evil.
Amen.

thy kingdom come,
thy will be done
on earth as it is in heaven.

6

3

Name: _____

**Dear Family,** Your child learned to walk and talk by imitating you. Your child also learns to pray by imitating you. Go for a walk together and comment on God's beauty. When you hear bad news on the TV, or sad news about a friend, or happy news, say a prayer with your child for the persons in need. No matter how or when you pray, invite your child to join you.

*RCLBenziger.com*

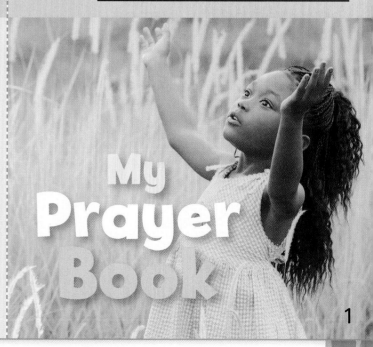

My Prayer Book

8

1

# We Praise and Thank God

Give us this day
our daily bread,

4

and forgive us our trespasses,
as we forgive those who trespass
against us;

5

Our Father, who art in heaven,
hallowed be thy name;

2

Draw a picture of yourself praying.

7

# Our Pope

The Pope is a friend of Jesus.

The Pope is the head of the Church.

The Pope helps us to pray.

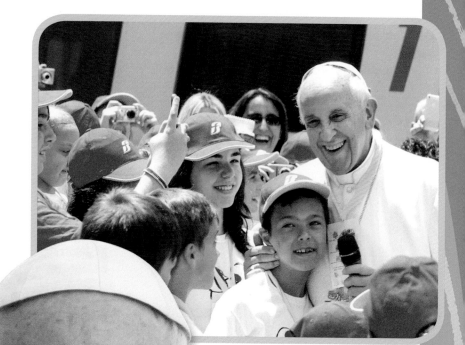

# Five-Finger Prayer

**Activity** Say a prayer for all God's people.
Use your fingers to help you.

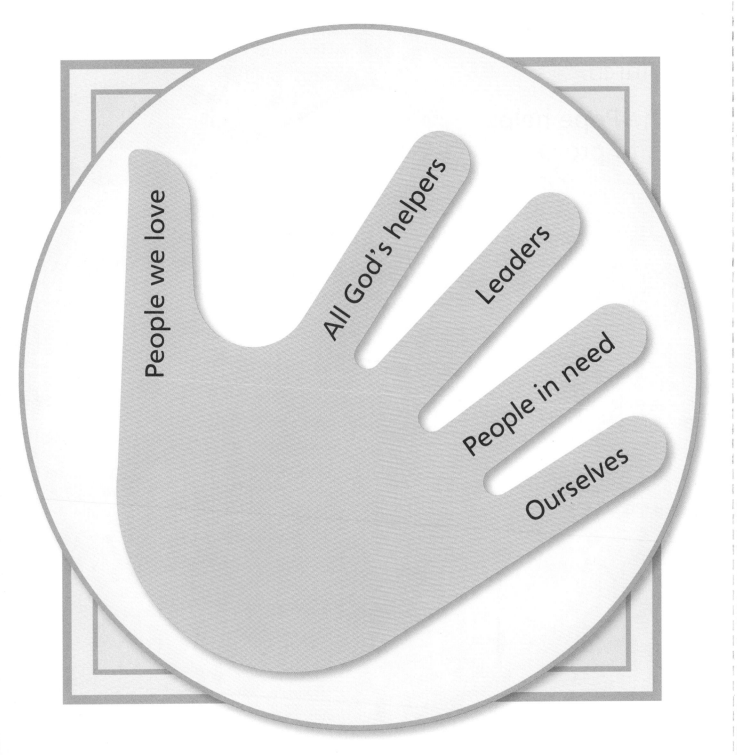

24

RCLBenziger.com ✳

Then Jesus embraced the children and blessed them, placing his hands on them.

*Based on Mark 10:1*

# My Bible

1

# Jesus Is Alive!

# Contents

22

# Easter

Jesus is not here.
*Based on Luke 24:1-12*

# God Creates the World

Genesis 1:1-31, 2:1-3

3

## Jesus at a Wedding

John 2:1-11

## Noah and the Ark

God saved Noah and his family.

God saved the animals.

# Jesus Tells Us About God

Matthew 5:43-45

God blessed the people.

God blessed the animals.

The rainbow was a sign.

God will care for all people and animals.

*Based on Genesis 7 and 8*

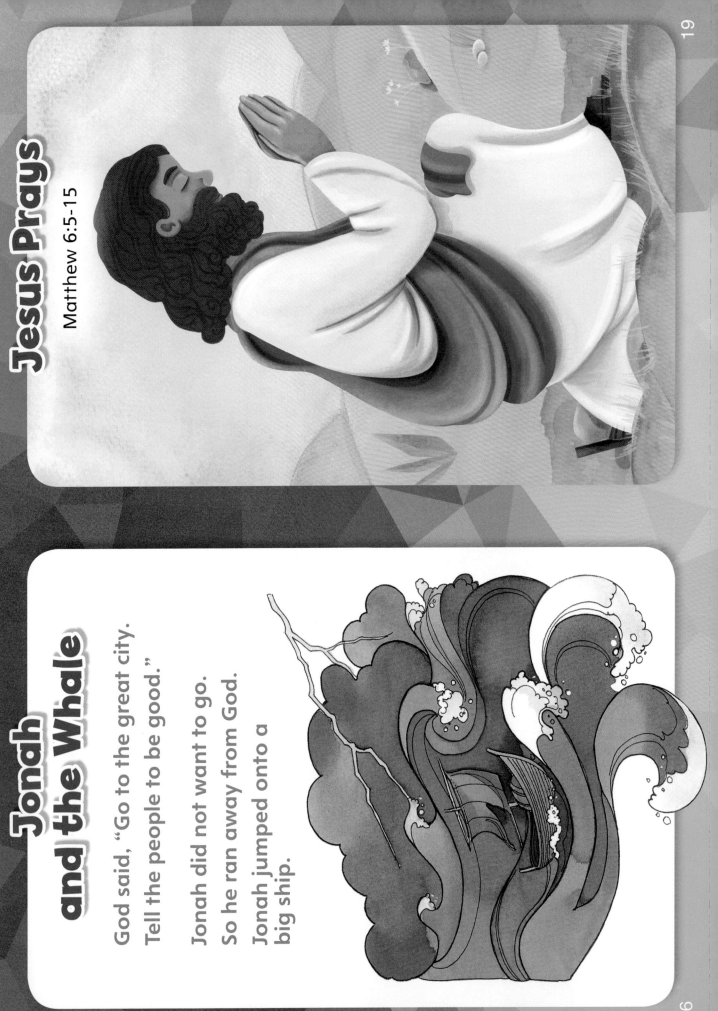

## Jesus Prays
Matthew 6:5-15

## Jonah and the Whale

God said, "Go to the great city.
Tell the people to be good."

Jonah did not want to go.
So he ran away from God.
Jonah jumped onto a big ship.

# Jesus Feeds the Hungry

Matthew 14:13-21

But God sent a big storm.
Jonah fell in the water.
A giant whale swallowed him.

Then the whale swam to the big city.
He spit Jonah out onto the shore.
Jonah repeated God's words.
The people obeyed and were happy.

*Based on Jonah 1-3*

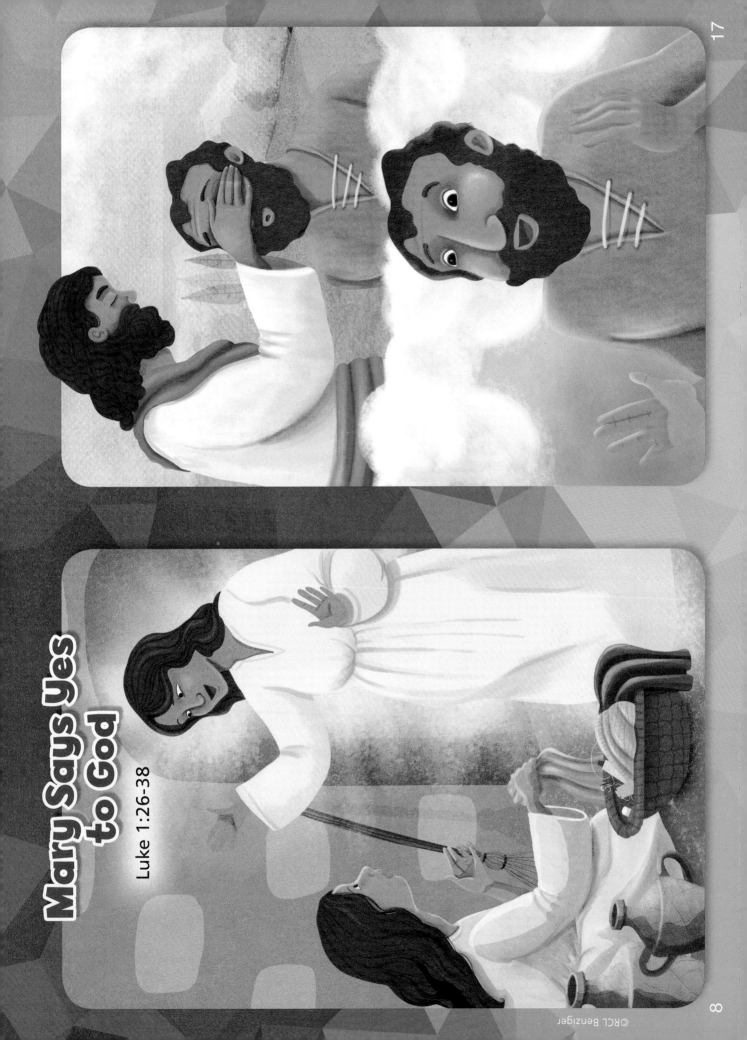

# Mary Says Yes to God

Luke 1:26-38

## Jesus Cures a Blind Man

Luke 18:35-43

## Jesus is Born

Matthew 2:1-14

# Jesus and the Children

Mark 10:13-16

# The Shepherds Adore Jesus

Matthew 2:15-20

## Jesus and His Apostles

Matthew 10:5-15

## Jesus Grows Up

Luke 2:39-40

# Jesus Gathers Friends

Matthew 2:15-20

# We Celebrate
# All Saints

Saints are special friends of God.

**Activity**

Read about Saints Isidore and Maria.

was a farmer.

He plowed the fields with an .

took care of the .

They loved their little .

helped .

She cooked for them.

went to a lot.

But he worked hard, too.

Then one day their little died.

and were so sad.

# We Celebrate All Saints

 and  asked God
to take care of their little .

Then they helped more .
They told the  about God's love.

With his ,  plowed for .
 made  for .

 and  loved God very much.
They helped  and were kind.

So the Church calls them saints.
They are saints  and .
They live with all the saints in Heaven.

All you saints of God, pray for us!

# We Celebrate
# Thanksgiving

Color the Thanksgiving picture.

# We Celebrate Thanksgiving

At Thanksgiving, we come together.
We give thanks to God.

**Activity** Fill the Thanksgiving plate with your favorite foods.

Draw yourself thanking God.

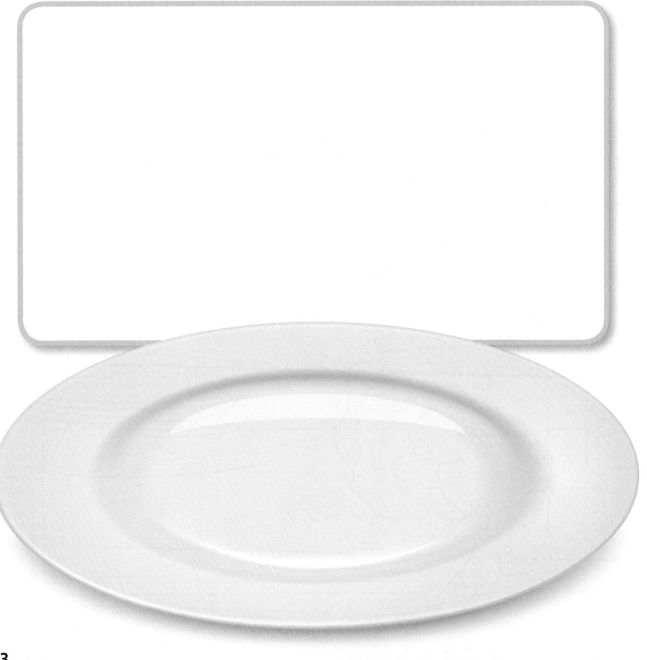

# We Celebrate Advent

**Activity** Color the squares to show times you have waited.

# We Wait for Jesus During Advent

Advent is here.

Jesus' birthday is near.

Get ready for Christmas to come.

**Activity** Glue the flames to light the Advent wreath.

# We Celebrate Advent

## A Take-Home Project

**Activity** Color the letters. Make an Advent wreath.

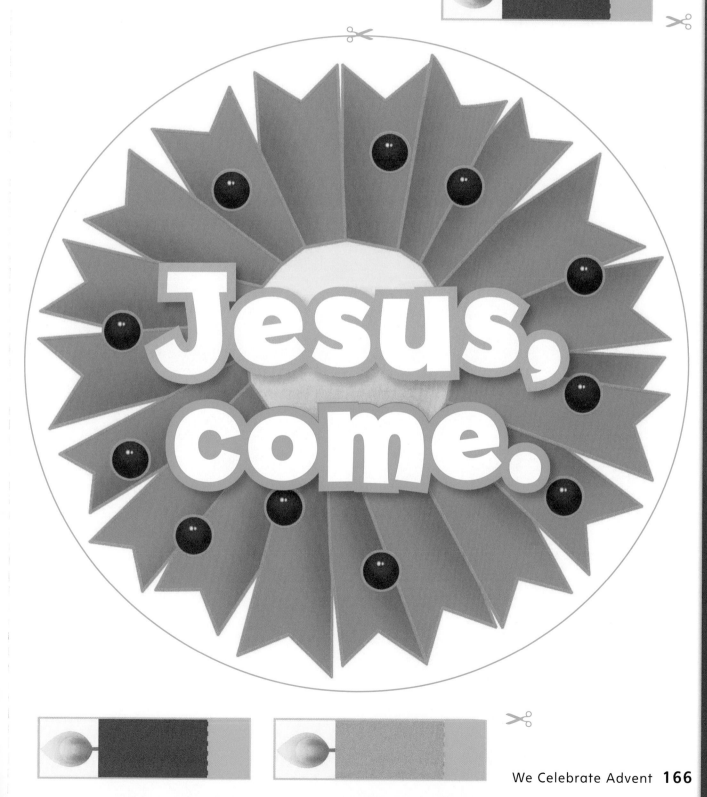

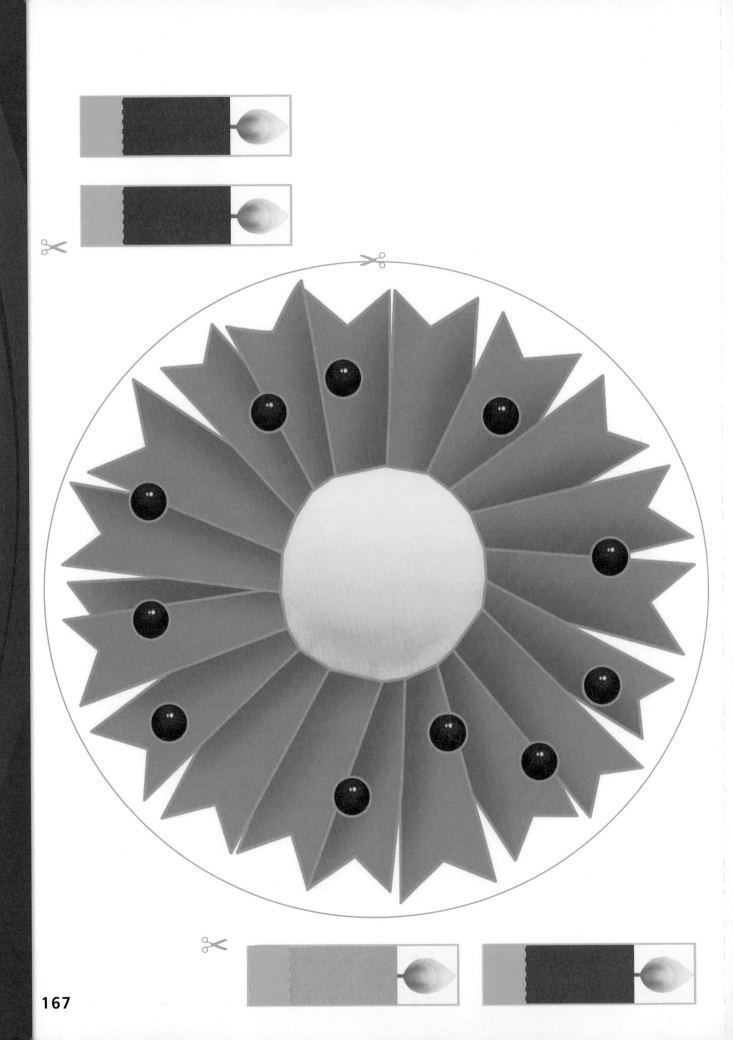

# We Celebrate Christmas

Jesus is God's gift to us.

**Activity** Glue yellow paper strips or pieces of straw to Jesus' manger.

## A Christmas Tree Helps Us Celebrate

**Activity** Decorate the Christmas tree.
Draw a gift to Jesus to put under the tree.

# The Christmas Story

Mary and Joseph went on a trip to Bethlehem.
Mary rode on a donkey.

They traveled the whole day long.
They were very tired.

The cold night was coming.
Joseph looked for a place to spend the night.
But there was no place to stay.

Then Mary and Joseph went into a stable.
The sheep were happy to see them.

During the night, Mary had a little baby.
She wrapped him up and held him close.

The shepherds heard about the baby.
They ran as fast as they could to the stable.

The shepherds saw the sleeping baby.
They whispered, "Praise God!"

Mary, Joseph, and the shepherds loved Jesus.
So do we, each and every day.

**Dear Family,**

Take time this Christmas to read together Luke 2:1-19, the Scripture account of the birth of Jesus and the visit of the shepherds.

# We Celebrate Valentine's Day

**Activity** Circle these valentine words in the puzzle.

friend    share    card    party    God

Use each word in a sentence.

## I Show My Love with Valentines

I will give valentines to these people.

Lent helps us grow as children of God.

**Activity** Cut out the flower you like.
Glue it in the box.

## We Grow During Lent

**Activity** Color a leaf when you share, care, or help.

I can share.

I can care.

I can help.

## ☙ A Story for Lent

Read the story.

One day, Jesus told a story.
A farmer planted grain.
Some grain fell on good ground.

Circle what the seed needs.

## The Grain of Wheat Changes

Suddenly, the grain changed and grew.

Up, up toward the sun it grew.

Soon it popped through the ground.

*Based on* John 12:24

Show what happened to the
grain of wheat.

At Easter we see signs of new life.

We remember that Jesus is alive.

Come and join the E_____ fun.

Brand new life has just begun.

## New Life Is All Around Us

**Activity**  Color the hidden butterflies.

## Jesus Is Risen! Alleluia!

Jesus died on Friday.
He was buried in a tomb.
A rock closed the tomb.

On Sunday, some women came.
They were surprised.
The rock was rolled back!

A man in a white robe stood there.
He said to them,
" . . . [Jesus] has been raised; he is not here."

Mark 16:6

Circle these words in the story.

Jesus      tomb      women      rock      raised

## "Alleluia" Is a Happy Word

 **Activity** Draw how you feel saying, "Alleluia!"

Mary is the mother of Jesus.
She is the Mother of God.
Mary is our mother too.

Families like to walk and play.
Who can tell us what they say?

## The Holy Family

The Holy Family loved one another.

**Activity** Color the picture of Jesus' family.

# The Holy Family Liked to Be Together

**Activity** Color the pictures.

Make a Holy Family stand.

Mary · Jesus · Joseph

We call Jesus, Mary, and Joseph the Holy Family.

Guess what Matthew and Pepper do together.

They play.

## Matthew and Pepper Are Friends

Tell the story about Matthew and Pepper.

## Friends Help One Another

**Activity** Draw how you would help Matthew.

## A Surprise for Matthew

Matthew was so sad.
Pepper was gone.
Matthew's dad hugged him.
He felt better.
Then Matthew remembered Pepper.
He felt sad again.

So Matthew took a walk.
Suddenly, a cat walked up to him.
The cat stretched and said, "Meow!"

"Go away, you pesky cat!" Matthew said.
But the cat followed Matthew home.

**Activity** Draw what happened next.

# We Celebrate
# New Beginnings

**Activity** Fill the backpack with new school things.

## A Prayer for First Grade

Color the letters.

Thank you, God, for new beginnings.

# We Celebrate with the Church

The Church year is a year of prayer.
It is a year of praise.

## Advent

Advent begins the Church year.
We get ready for the birth of Jesus.
The color for Advent is purple.

## Christmas

Christmas is when Jesus was born.
The color for Christmas is white.

## Lent

Lent helps us grow as children of God.
We remember that Jesus died for us.
We get ready for Easter.
The color for Lent is purple.

## Easter

Easter means that Jesus lives.
Jesus gave us the gift of new life.
The color for Easter is white.

## Ordinary Time

Ordinary Time is the longest time
of the Church year.
We learn more stories about Jesus.
The color for Ordinary Time is green.

# We Celebrate
## Saints

Saints are friends of God.

Saints follow Jesus.

Saints help us follow Jesus.

We can pray to the saints.

**Activity**

Draw one way you follow Jesus like the saints.

**Pray:**
All the saints, pray for us.
Amen.

## Saint Elizabeth Ann Seton

Elizabeth was a wife and mother.

She started schools to help the poor.

She started homes for children with no families.

Saint Elizabeth Ann Seton was the first saint born in America.

**Pray:**
Saint Elizabeth Ann Seton, pray for us. Amen.

## Saint Francis of Assisi

Francis loved God.

He loved all God's creation.

Francis loved the animals big and small.

He told everyone, "Praise the Lord!"

**Pray:**
Saint Francis of Assisi, pray for us. Amen.

## Saint Joseph

Joseph was the husband of Mary.

Joseph loved Mary and Jesus.

**Pray:**
Saint Joseph,
pray for us. Amen.

## Saint Julie Billiart

Julie was a Sister. She taught others about God.

She taught them to teach religion.

She taught children to know and love God.

**Pray:**
Saint Julie Billiart,
pray for us. Amen.

## Saint Kateri

Kateri was a Native American.

She taught children about God.

She cared for people who were sick and old.

**Pray:**
Saint Kateri,
pray for us. Amen.

## Our Lady of Guadalupe

Mary, the mother of Jesus has many titles.

One title that we call Mary is Our Lady of Guadalupe.

One day in Mexico, Mary appeared to Juan Diego.

She told Juan to ask her for help.

Mary will help us if we ask too.

**Pray:**
Our Lady of Guadalupe,
pray for us. Amen.

# We Pray

## The Sign of the Cross

In the name of the Father,

and of the Son,

and of the Holy

Spirit.

Amen.

## The Our Father

Our Father, who art in heaven,
hallowed be thy name;
thy kingdom come,
thy will be done
on earth as it is in heaven.
Give us this day our daily bread,
and forgive us our trespasses,
as we forgive those who
   trespass against us;
and lead us not into temptation,
but deliver us from evil.
Amen.

# We Pray

## The Hail Mary

Hail, Mary, full of grace,
the Lord is with thee.
Blessed art thou
    among women
and blessed is the fruit
    of thy womb, Jesus.
Holy Mary, Mother of God,
pray for us sinners,
now and at the hour of
    our death.
Amen.

## Glory Be

Glory be to the Father
and to the Son
and to the Holy Spirit,
as it was in the beginning
is now, and ever shall be
world without end.
Amen.

## Angel of God

Angel of God,
my guardian dear,
to whom God's love
    commits me here,
ever this day be at my side,
to light and guard, to rule
    and guide.
Amen.

## Morning Prayer

Dear God, as I begin
    this day,
Keep me in your love
    and care.
Help me to live as your
    child today.
Bless me, my family, and
    my friends in all I do.
Keep us close to you.
Amen.

## Evening Prayer

Dear God,
I thank you for today.
Keep me safe
    throughout the night.
Thank you for all the
    good I did today.
I am sorry for what
    I have chosen to
    do wrong.
Bless my family and
    my friends.
Amen.

## Grace Before Meals

Bless us, O Lord,
and these thy gifts,
which we are about to
receive from thy bounty,
through Christ our Lord.
Amen.

## Grace After Meals

We give thee thanks
for all thy benefits,
almighty God,
who lives and
reigns forever.
Amen.

## A Prayer to Follow Jesus

God, I know you will call me for
   special work in my life.
Help me follow Jesus each day and
   be ready to answer your call.
Amen.

## The Great Commandment

"You shall love the Lord,
your God, with all your
heart, with all your soul,
and with all your mind. . . .
You shall love your neighbor as yourself."

Matthew 22:37, 39

# Credits

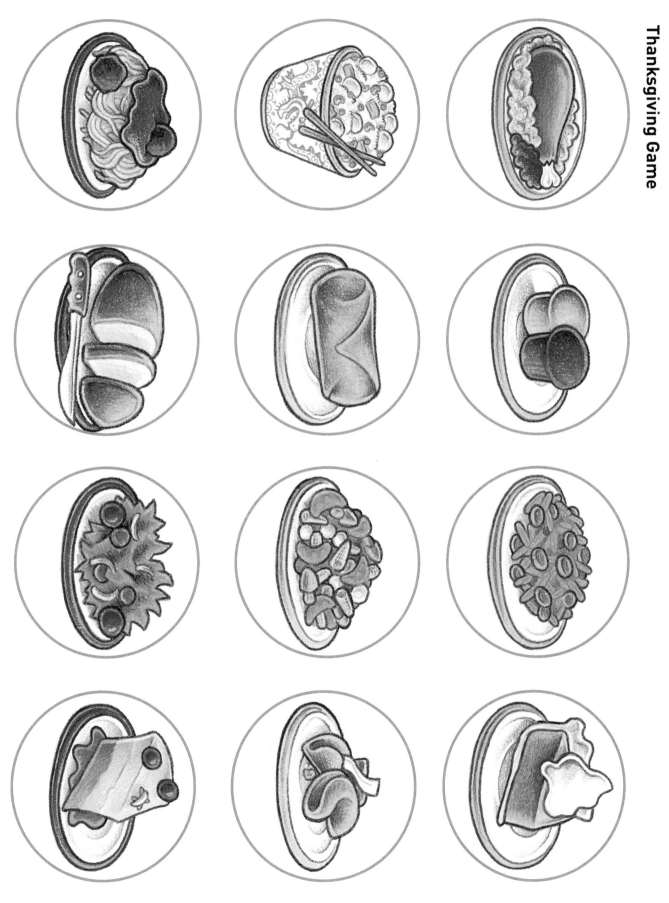

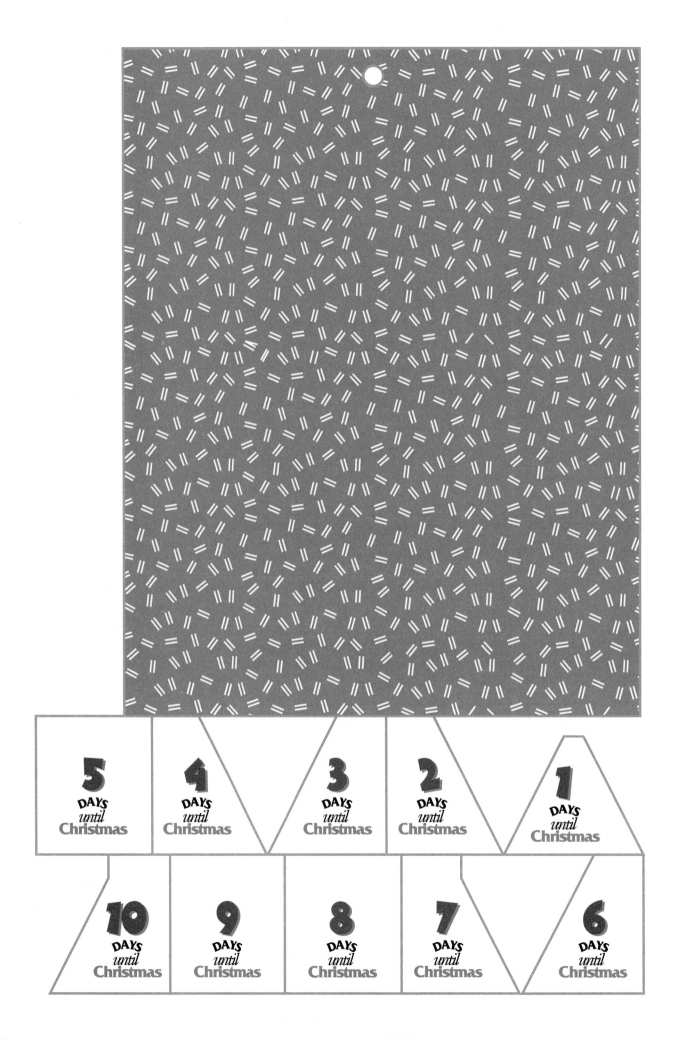

**5**
DAYS
*until*
Christmas

**4**
DAYS
*until*
Christmas

**3**
DAYS
*until*
Christmas

**2**
DAYS
*until*
Christmas

**1**
DAYS
*until*
Christmas

**10**
DAYS
*until*
Christmas

**9**
DAYS
*until*
Christmas

**8**
DAYS
*until*
Christmas

**7**
DAYS
*until*
Christmas

**6**
DAYS
*until*
Christmas

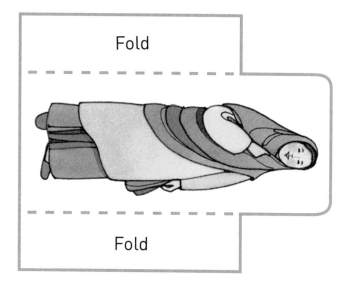

Fold

Fold

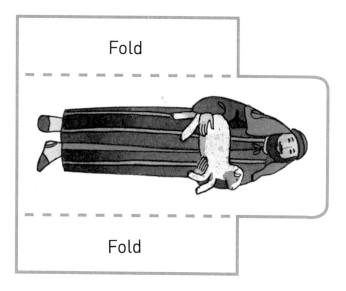

Fold

Fold

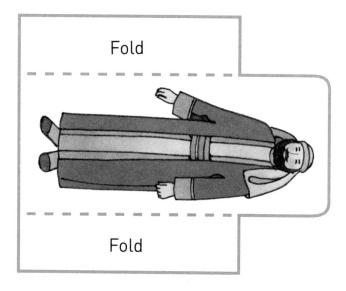

Fold

Fold

Fold

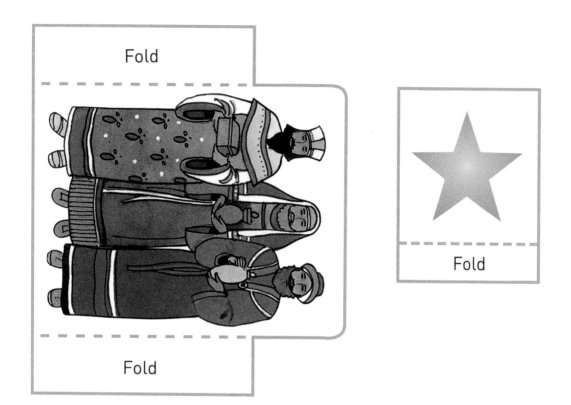

Fold

Fold

Fold

Fold

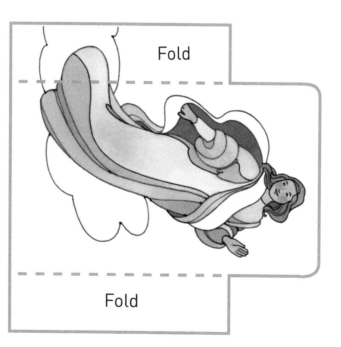

Fold

Fold

**Spinner**

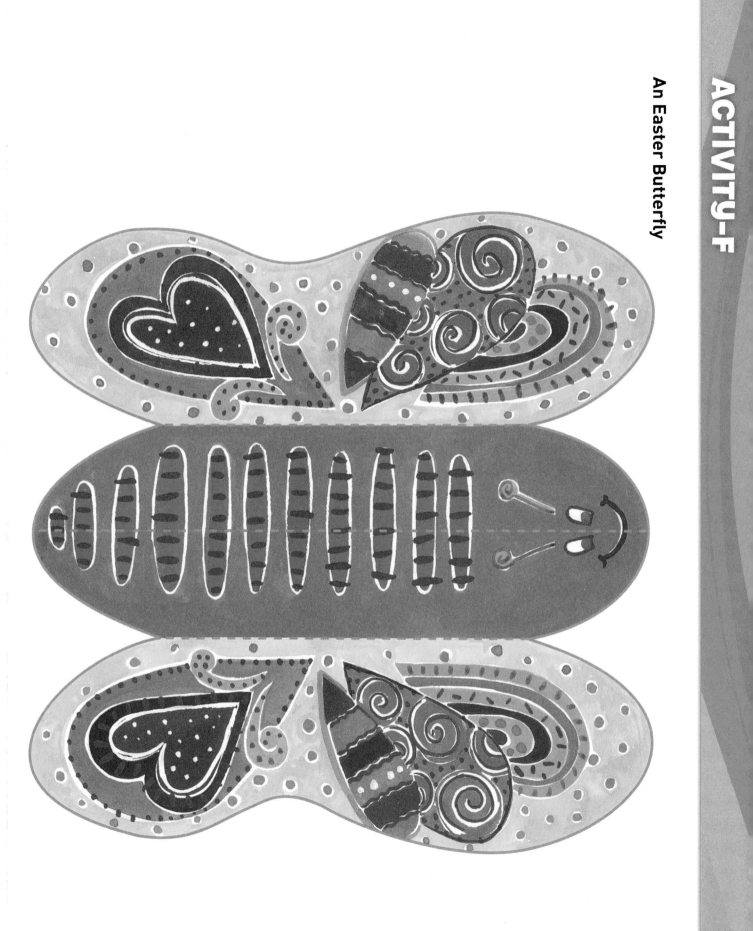

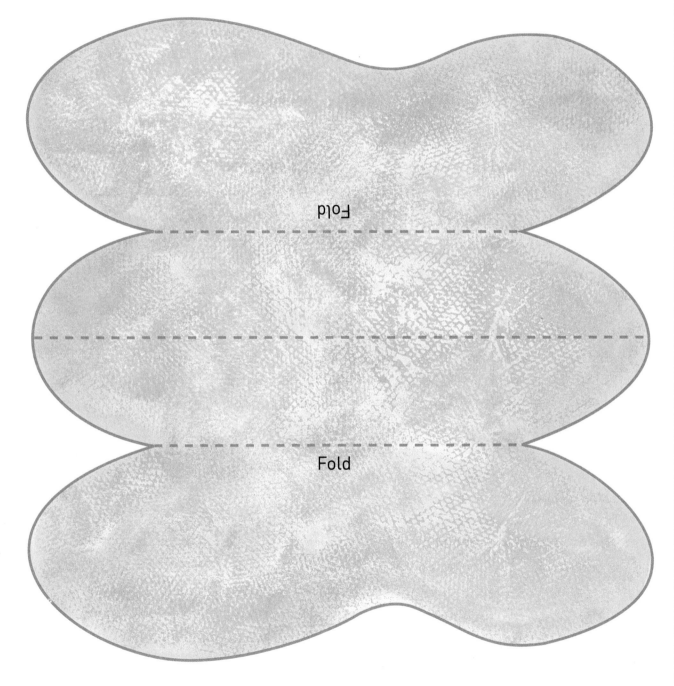

**A Lenten Cocoon**

Fold

Fold

Fold

# Congratulations

NAME _____

## on how you have grown this year!

Draw
what
you can
do now.